WHO WERE THE

ANCIENT EGYPTIANS?

First published in 2006
in the UK by Franklin Watts
338 Euston Road, London NW1 3BH

Franklin Watts Australia, Hachette Children's Books
Level 17/207 Kent Street, Sydney NSW 2000

This series was devised and produced by McRae Books Srl,
Borgo S. Croce, 8, Florence (Italy)

Publishers: Anne McRae and Marco Nardi
Text: Loredana Agosta, Anne McRae
Main Illustrations: MM comunicazione
(Manuela Cappon, Monica Favilli),
Antonella Pastorelli, Paola Ravaglia

Illustrations: Lorenzo Cecchi, Studio Stalio (Alessandro
Cantucci, Fabiano Fabbrucci, Margherita Salvadori)

Design: Marco Nardi
Colour separations: Fotolito Toscana, Firenze

© 2006 McRae Books Srl, Florence
A CIP catalogue record for this book is available
from the British Library.
Dewey Decimal Classification Number: 938

ISBN 0 7496 6790 7
ISBN-13 978 0 7496 6790 0

Printed and bound in Italy.

WHO WERE THE
ANCIENT EGYPTIANS?

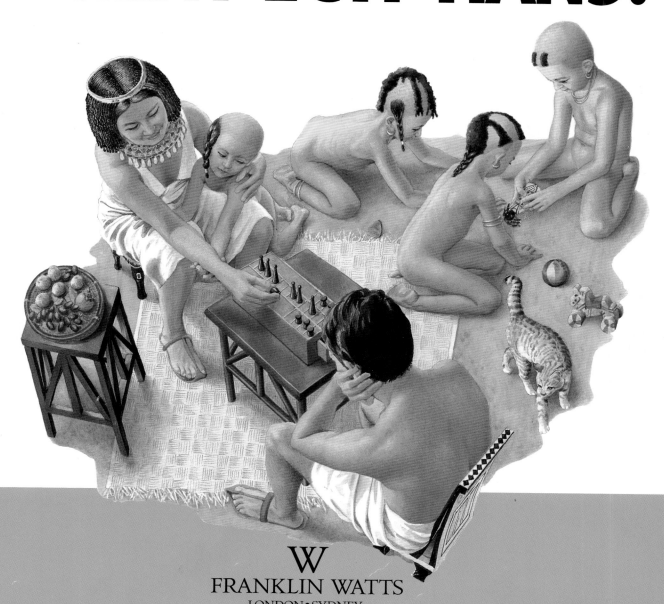

W

FRANKLIN WATTS

LONDON • SYDNEY

Pyramids
see pages 12-13

Origins
see pages 8-9

Jewellery
see page 28

Ancient Egypt

The Egyptian Empire
at its greatest extent

MEDITERRANEAN SEA

LEVANT

• Byblos

• Gaza

Avaris •

Memphis •

SINAI

• Akhetaten
(El-Amarna)

River Nile

*Valley of
the Kings*
• Thebes

RED SEA

• Elephantine

NUBIA

KUSH

• Napata

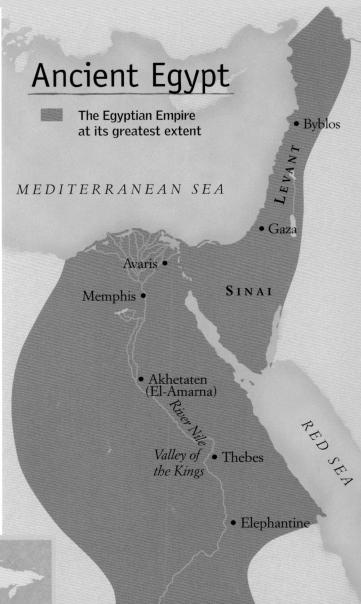

World Map

Art see pages 18-19

Feasts and Festivals see pages 22-23

Contents

Trade
see pages
30-31

Royal Duties
see pages 14-15

The River Nile
see pages
10-11

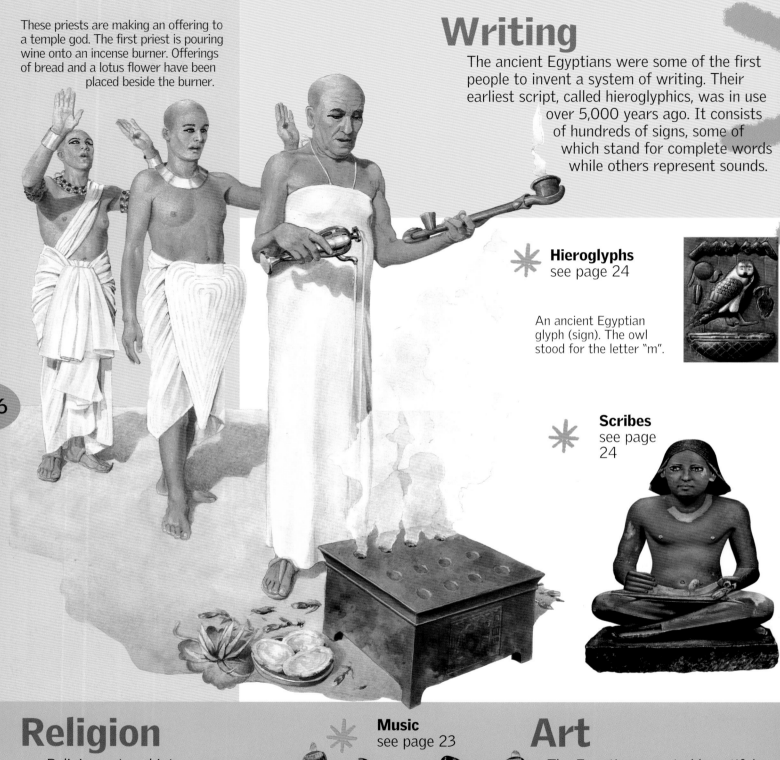

These priests are making an offering to a temple god. The first priest is pouring wine onto an incense burner. Offerings of bread and a lotus flower have been placed beside the burner.

Writing

The ancient Egyptians were some of the first people to invent a system of writing. Their earliest script, called hieroglyphics, was in use over 5,000 years ago. It consists of hundreds of signs, some of which stand for complete words while others represent sounds.

✳ Hieroglyphs
see page 24

An ancient Egyptian glyph (sign). The owl stood for the letter "m".

✳ Scribes
see page 24

6

Religion

Religion entered into every aspect of life in ancient Egypt. There were gods and goddesses for almost everything and religious rituals were a part of daily life. Major festivals were held at temples and presided over by priests.

✳ Music
see page 23

Art

The Egyptians created beautiful paintings, statues and other works of art. Many of these have survived. Much of what we know about the ancient Egyptians is based on the study of these works.

This detail from a wall painting shows women playing various musical instruments.

Divine Leaders

The Egyptians believed that their pharaohs (kings) were gods who should rule over all of Egypt with absolute power. At many times in the long history of Egyptian civilization they also ruled a large foreign empire.

The mask of Tutankhamun, perhaps the most well-known pharaoh in Egyptian history. His burial place was uncovered in 1922.

 Pharaohs
see pages 14-15

Egyptian farmers used simple tools to prepare their fields for the crops they sowed after the Nile floodwaters retreated.

 Cereals
see page 27

Who were the ancient Egyptians?

The ancient Egyptians were an African people who built a great civilization that flourished along the River Nile in Egypt for more than 3,000 years. Egypt was ruled by kings, called pharaohs, who governed the narrow country efficiently, keeping it united and undertaking great building projects. Most Egyptians lived simple lives, working as farmers and caring for their families. A few people became priests, scribes and officials of the state.

7

The Nile

The River Nile rises in Central Africa and Ethiopia and runs almost 6,500 km (400 miles) to the Mediterranean Sea. It was the lifeblood of Egypt, and Egyptian civilization would not have been possible without it.

Mummies
see page 16

 **Trade**
see pages 30-31

The goddess Selket was the protector of mummies. Many precious objects, like this golden statue of the goddess, were found in the tombs of the pharaohs.

This scene shows men carrying grain off a river boat and trading it at a market.

This red bowl decorated with white Nile crocodiles was made in about 4000 BC.

Before the Pharaohs

The time before the rule of the first pharaoh is known as the Predynastic era. Information about Egypt in those prehistoric times, before writing was invented, comes from archaeological finds, such as tools and pottery.

By the time of the First Dynasties, the ancient Egyptians were already skilled craftspeople. This beautiful stone vase with a gold rim dates from then.

Early settlers along the Nile built homes out of bricks made by combining mud, straw and sand. The bricks were then left out in the sun to harden.

The First Dynasties

The First Dynasties period began with the reign of Narmer in about 3150 BC. He was the first pharaoh to rule both Upper and Lower Egypt. According to legend, Menes united the two kingdoms and became the first pharaoh. Some believe that Narmer is associated with this legendary ruler and that they are the same person. The second pharaoh of united Egypt was probably Narmer's son.

Narmer is depicted holding down a prisoner on this carved stone tablet.

The Old Kingdom

Egypt was rich and powerful during the 500-year period known as The Old Kingdom. Almost all the pyramids were erected at this time, including the largest ever built at Giza. Failure of the annual Nile floods caused a famine that ended the Old Kingdom.

Egypt was divided once more for over 140 years, a time called the First Intermediate period.

An Old Kingdom pharaoh, Menkaure, stands between two goddesses.

Origins

The Nile Valley has been inhabited for thousands of years. About 8,000 years ago early farmers founded small settlements along the Nile. These grew into villages which eventually gave rise to the two separate kingdoms of Upper and Lower Egypt. These lands were united when the pharaoh of Upper Egypt conquered Lower Egypt and established the capital city at Memphis.

Timeline

Ancient Egyptian history can be divided into periods by grouping together dynasties, or periods, during which a line of rulers coming from the same family ruled. This timeline shows the main periods in ancient Egyptian history.

Predynastic era
c.5500–3150 BC

First Dynasties period
3150–2686 BC

Old Kingdom period
2686–2181 BC

First Intermediate period
2181–2040 BC

Middle Kingdom period
2040–1782 BC

Second Intermediate period
1782–1570 BC

New Kingdom period
1570–1070 BC

Third Intermediate period
1070–664 BC

Late period
664–332 BC

Greek and Roman period
332 BC–AD 641

The god Horus was believed to be the protector of pharaohs. He is often shown as a falcon in Egyptian art.

Upper and Lower Egypt

Lower Egypt covered the lowlands of the Nile delta, where the river fans out into many branches. Upper Egypt was the narrow strip of land that ran along the banks of the River Nile. Memphis, the first capital of united Egypt, was located on the Nile just north of the delta (only slightly further north than modern-day Cairo). It was the ideal position from which to rule both kingdoms.

The pharaoh's crown bore a vulture, the symbol of Upper Egypt, and a cobra, the symbol of Lower Egypt.

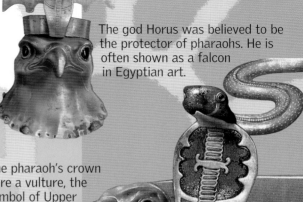

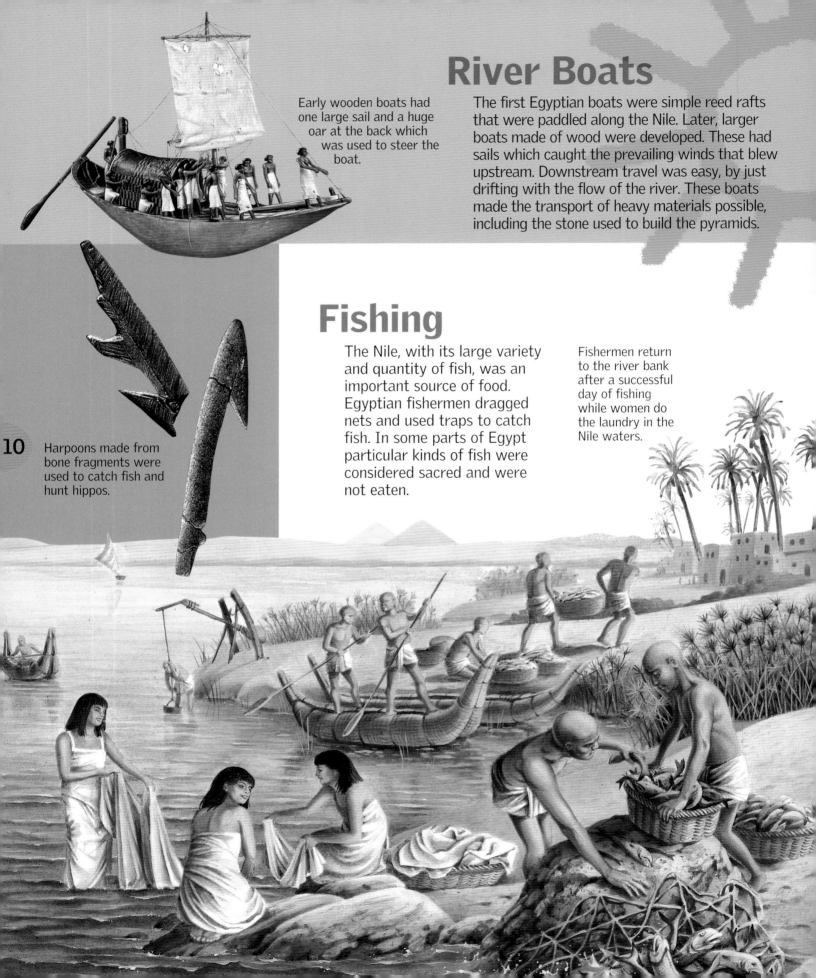

River Boats

Early wooden boats had one large sail and a huge oar at the back which was used to steer the boat.

The first Egyptian boats were simple reed rafts that were paddled along the Nile. Later, larger boats made of wood were developed. These had sails which caught the prevailing winds that blew upstream. Downstream travel was easy, by just drifting with the flow of the river. These boats made the transport of heavy materials possible, including the stone used to build the pyramids.

Fishing

The Nile, with its large variety and quantity of fish, was an important source of food. Egyptian fishermen dragged nets and used traps to catch fish. In some parts of Egypt particular kinds of fish were considered sacred and were not eaten.

Fishermen return to the river bank after a successful day of fishing while women do the laundry in the Nile waters.

Harpoons made from bone fragments were used to catch fish and hunt hippos.

Good Years and Bad

Wild hippos that lived by the river caused damage to crops.

Egypt was dependent on the regular flooding of the Nile. But some years the flood was too high and it swept away entire villages. Other years it was too low so that the rich farmlands turned to dust and the people starved. The Egyptians made offerings to the gods asking for regular floods.

The River Nile is shown here as a blue man, covered in waves. He is holding a palm rib, the hieroglyph (sign) for "year" which symbolised the annual flood.

River of Life

Almost all of ancient Egypt was covered in arid desert except for the lush Nile Valley. Every summer the River Nile flooded its banks, depositing rich dark silt along the river valley. The Egyptians called this "The Black Land" and it was one of the most fertile regions on Earth. Here they grew an abundance of food and it was the basis of their civilization. The river itself was an important source of food and water, as well as a place to bathe and wash clothing. It was also the main route for trade and transport.

Flooding

The River Nile flooded every summer because of the monsoon rains that fell far upstream, in modern Ethiopia. Although the Egyptians did not know why the floods came, they learned to predict their regular appearance. The annual cycle of the Nile was the basis for their calendar.

This painted fragment shows a calf playing among the plants on the river bank.

Plants and Animals

Two important plants that grew along the banks of the Nile were papyrus and flax. The reeds of the papyrus plant were used to make rope, mats, boxes and scrolls used for writing. Flax was used to make linen; almost all Egyptian clothing was made of white linen. The wild animals of the river included ferocious hippos (now extinct on the Nile) and crocodiles, as well as frogs, snakes and mosquitoes.

One of the earliest pyramids was the step pyramid at Saqqara, built by the royal architect Imhotep for the pharaoh Djoser of the third dynasty.

Fit For Royalty

The dead pharaoh's body was brought to the pyramid site on a boat. It was then made into a mummy before being buried in a tomb inside the pyramid. Many people lived in the area around the pyramids. Initially, there were builders, both workers and skilled craftspeople, and later priests and special servants. Villages grew up to support these people.

Technical Skill

The Egyptians were skilled engineers and superb stonemasons. The first archaeologists to study the pyramids were astounded by the accuracy of their measurements. Great technical knowledge was required to build such big, solid structures and good organisation was needed to ensure they were completed.

Pyramid
Builders

During the Old Kingdom the most powerful pharaohs built huge pyramids to be used as their tombs when they died. The largest, called the Great Pyramid, is one of the heaviest structures ever built. Made to order by the pharaoh Khufu, more than 2.3 million giant blocks of stone were carried to the site at Giza and carefully fitted together. More than 40 centuries after they were built, many pyramids are still standing.

The Great Sphinx

The vast stone sculpture of a sphinx (a creature with a human head and a lion's body) that still stands at Giza is part of the pyramid complex of the pharaoh Khafre. The sphinx is thought to represent the sun god Re-Harakhte, while its face is a portrait of Khafre. The sphinx was one of many hundreds of statues built during Khafre's reign.

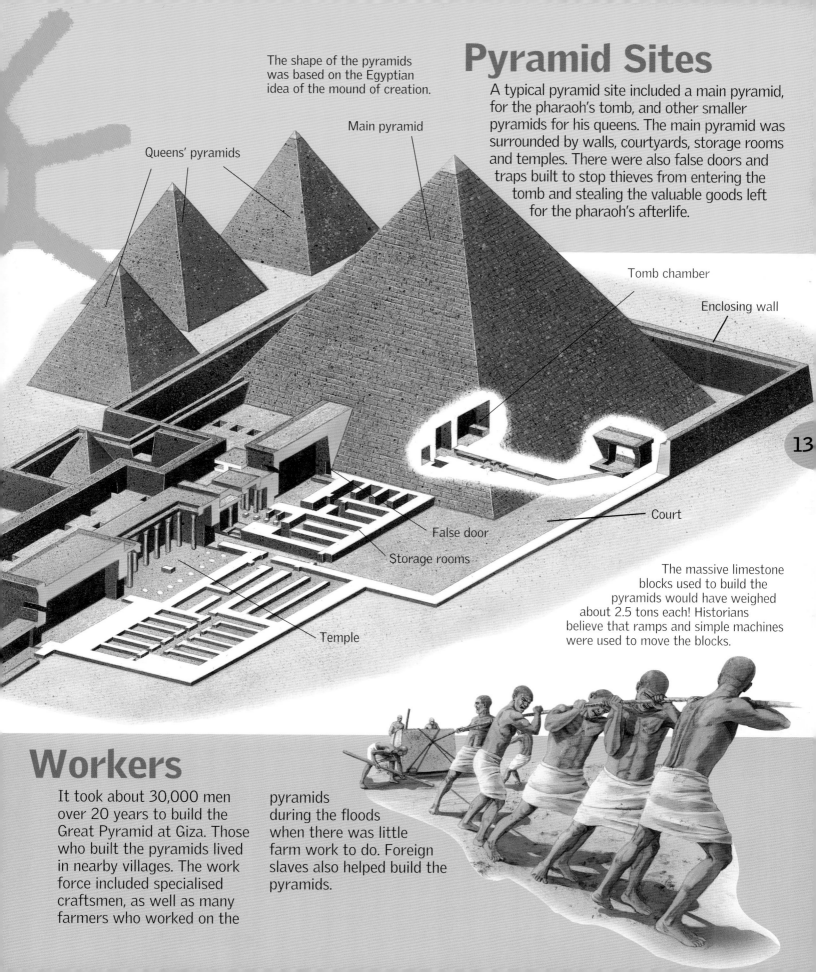

The shape of the pyramids was based on the Egyptian idea of the mound of creation.

Pyramid Sites

A typical pyramid site included a main pyramid, for the pharaoh's tomb, and other smaller pyramids for his queens. The main pyramid was surrounded by walls, courtyards, storage rooms and temples. There were also false doors and traps built to stop thieves from entering the tomb and stealing the valuable goods left for the pharaoh's afterlife.

Queens' pyramids

Main pyramid

Tomb chamber

Enclosing wall

Court

False door

Storage rooms

Temple

The massive limestone blocks used to build the pyramids would have weighed about 2.5 tons each! Historians believe that ramps and simple machines were used to move the blocks.

Workers

It took about 30,000 men over 20 years to build the Great Pyramid at Giza. Those who built the pyramids lived in nearby villages. The work force included specialised craftsmen, as well as many farmers who worked on the pyramids during the floods when there was little farm work to do. Foreign slaves also helped build the pyramids.

Royal Women

Both the pharaoh's mother and principal wife played important roles in rituals and were probably considered divine. Royal women could not inherit the throne, even if there was no male heir to take it. However, a few women did gain power, usually through their sons. One queen, Hatsheput, is recorded as "mistress of the two lands" and seems to have ruled as pharaoh.

Queen Tiy had great influence over her son, Akhenaten, when he became pharaoh.

Pharaohs
and Queens

Egyptian pharaohs were very powerful. They ruled over every aspect of Egyptian life, from running the government and the army, to deciding all religious matters. From Old Kingdom times onwards they were treated as gods. Most pharaohs had a principal wife, whose son usually became the next pharaoh, as well as several minor wives. The pharaoh's mother was also treated as a queen.

A statue of the pharaoh Tuthmosis IV, making an offering to the gods.

We know about Egyptian pharaohs because many of them left lists with the names of their ancestors. They often included dates and important events.

14

Pharaohs are often shown wearing special clothes or holding symbols of their power. These are some of the most common symbols.

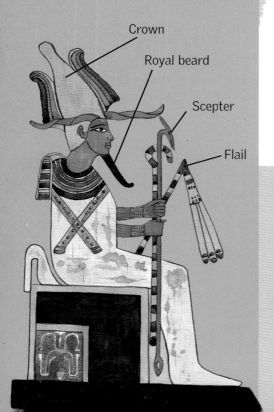

Crown

Royal beard

Scepter

Flail

Chief Priest

As high priest the pharaoh had to make sure that the gods and goddesses were worshipped in the correct way. He ordered the building of temples and the making of offerings. Also, as spiritual leader, he had to maintain justice and order to preserve peace and prosperity.

Royal Duties

The pharaoh's most important job was to keep Egypt peaceful and wealthy. He was head of the army and was expected to protect the country against enemies. He also had to make sure that Egypt was properly governed and that taxes were paid.

Officials

The pharaoh had so many duties that he needed many officials to help him. Egypt was divided into provinces run by local governors. They represented the pharaoh and collected taxes for him. The vizier, or chief minister, was the top state official and he reported directly to the pharaoh.

A copy of a wall painting showing Ramesses II fighting the Hittites. As usual in Egyptian art, the pharaoh is shown very large while his tiny enemies are trampled underfoot.

15

This bronze statue shows a vizier in his official clothing – a long apron kilt with a special strap.

Gods and Goddesses

Some of the most well-known gods and goddesses were Amun-Ra (the creator of Egypt), Isis (wife of Osiris and mother of Horus), Anubis (god of the dead and mummy-making), Hathor (sky goddess) and Bastet (cat goddess associated with the moon and daughter of the sun god).

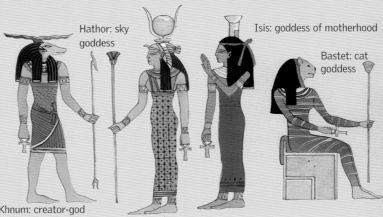

Hathor: sky goddess

Isis: goddess of motherhood

Bastet: cat goddess

Khnum: creator-god

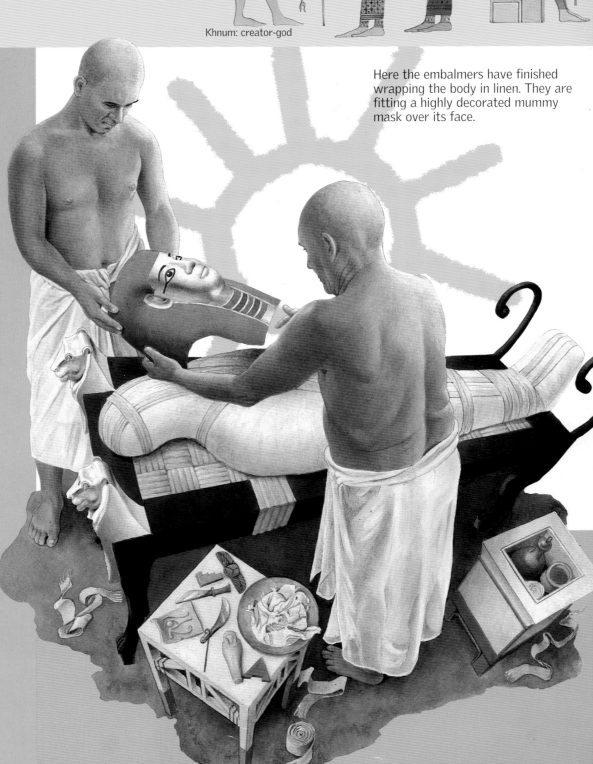

Here the embalmers have finished wrapping the body in linen. They are fitting a highly decorated mummy mask over its face.

Afterlife

The Egyptians firmly believed in life after death. They began preparing for the afterlife many years before they died. The wealthy had elaborate tombs built and arranged for their bodies to be preserved as mummies. The mummy was meant to be a home for the person's spirit in the afterlife.

16

Mummies

Making a body into a mummy was a long and elaborate process. First, the brain was sucked out of the head through the nostrils. Then, all the internal organs, except the heart, were removed and placed in special jars. The body was then packed in salt and left for 40 days. Finally, it was wrapped in linen and placed in a coffin.

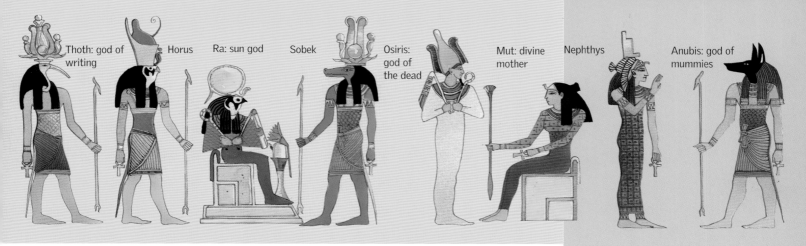

Thoth: god of writing   Horus   Ra: sun god   Sobek   Osiris: god of the dead   Mut: divine mother   Nephthys   Anubis: god of mummies

Religion

Maat was shown as a kneeling woman with an ostrich feather in her hair.

Religion was an important part of daily life in Egypt. There were many gods and goddesses, each associated with a place, animal, event or moment in life. For example Isis, goddess of motherhood, was called on during childbirth to protect the mother and her baby. People worshipped in private at wayside shrines or in their homes. They also brought gifts to temples dedicated to a particular god or goddess. However, they were not allowed to enter – only the priests went inside.

Chaos and Order

The Egyptians believed that life was a constant struggle between chaos and order. Maat, goddess of truth and justice and sister of the pharaohs, represented harmony and the correct order of things in the world.

Creation

According to Egyptian mythology, the world began when Amun-Ra rose up from a watery chaos and created Shu, the god of air, and Tefnut, the goddess of dew and moisture. Shu and Tefnut created Geb, the Earth god, and Nut, the sky goddess. The children of Geb and Nut were Osiris, Seth, Isis and Nephthys. They lived on Earth and many other gods were born after them.

Nut, the Egyptian sky-goddess, is covered in stars. She arches over the earth-god, her brother Geb.

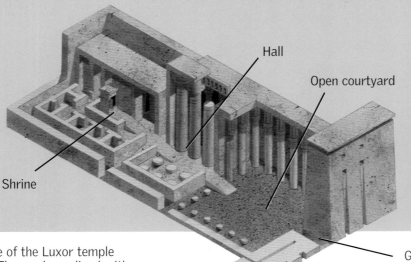

Most temples were built to a similar plan, with a gateway, open courtyard, a hall with columns and a shrine.

Hall

Open courtyard

Shrine

Gateway

The relief carving above shows a row of priests carrying offerings for the deceased.

The main entrance of the Luxor temple was magnificent. The road was lined with 365 statues of sphinxes and two tall obelisks stood on either side of the main door. At festival time the statues of Amun and Mut were paraded through the doors into the temple.

Temples

The first temples were simple mud-brick structures built to house the shrine of a god or goddess. Not many of these have survived. During the New Kingdom the Egyptians built much larger temples with splendid gateways, courtyards and halls with columns.

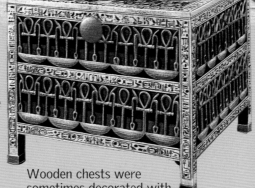

Wooden chests were sometimes decorated with ivory, silver and gold.

Crafts

Carpenters and craftspeople used wood and metals to make household objects for everyday use. Wealthy people could afford to have these richly decorated and many of these objects have been preserved since they were placed in tombs.

Sculpture

Egyptian artists made statues from the earliest times. Many showed deities or pharaohs, but wealthy or important people were also shown. The sculptors used sandstone, granite, wood, limestone and other hard substances. Many sculptures were brightly painted.

This bust of Queen Nefertiti is made from painted limestone.

Gold

Gold was a favourite metal and goldsmiths beat or cast it to make or decorate statues, jewellery, furniture and many other decorative objects.

Goldsmiths used thin sheets of gold to cover objects like this statuette showing the pharaoh Tutankhamun on a raft.

Art
and Architecture

The Egyptians made beautiful statues and paintings and built large, richly decorated temples, pyramids and tombs. These works of art were almost always created to celebrate a god or goddess, or in praise of the pharaoh and his family. Skilled craftspeople made fine jewellery and household objects using wood, glass, ceramics and precious stones.

This detailed painting shows a scribe with his wife and daughter, and their cat, as they hunt birds.

Painting

Egyptian artists left thousands of vividly coloured paintings. Most of the ones that have survived come from New Kingdom tombs. Many have religious themes while others show daily life. Painting styles did not change much over time. Human figures are almost all shown in the same way with their heads in profile (side on) and their shoulders straight on.

Axes used by foot soldiers in close combat were made with wooden handles and bronze blades.

Weapons

Charioteers and foot soldiers were armed with wooden bows and arrows, axes and clubs. Arrowheads were made of flint, a stone that can be filed into razor sharp edges. Later, as metalworking advanced, flint was replaced with bronze and swords and daggers were also made.

Some weapons were made for ceremonial purposes. This axe, richly decorated with gold and precious stones, belonged to the pharaoh Ahmose I.

Warriors
and War

Prisoners

Like many other peoples in the ancient world, the Egyptians believed that they were superior to all others. Captives taken in battle were forced into slave labour and made up a large part of the work force used to build Egyptian monuments.

Images of bound prisoners decorated many temples. They were made to emphasise the greatness of Egypt's power.

The desert and the sea provided natural defences for Egypt, making it hard to attack. So, in early times, only a small army was needed. During the New Kingdom period, a much larger army of professional soldiers was created. This army helped to protect Egypt from invasion and made it possible to conquer foreign lands as ambitious pharaohs expanded Egypt's boundaries.

Soldiers

Armies were mostly made up of mercenaries, soldiers who were paid to fight. The Egyptians hired some specialist charioteers and bowmen from Nubia and Libya. In later times, some soldiers were prisoners-of-war who served in the army to win their freedom.

This detail from a painting found on a coffin shows an Egyptian taking on four Nubians.

Empire!

Some of the later pharaohs believed they had the right to rule all the lands of the world. They expanded south, into Nubia, which was rich in gold, and east into the Near East. The Empire reached its greatest extent in the New Kingdom after long, hard military campaigns. But keeping an empire was expensive and Egypt soon shrank back to its natural borders.

Archers wore bracers on their wrists to protect them from the bowstring when shooting arrows. This ivory one shows a god watching a pharaoh striking an enemy.

Egypt faced one of its greatest threats with the invasion of the "sea peoples" during the reign of Ramesses III. Although the Egyptians were able to resist attack, the New Kingdom was seriously weakened.

Great Battles

The Battle of Qadesh, fought in modern-day Syria in 1294 BC, was one of the greatest battles in Egyptian history. Ramesses II led 20,000 men into war against the Hittite king, Muwatalis. History is divided about the outcome, although both rulers claimed to have won. In any case we know that the Egyptians suffered great loss of life.

This model showing Egyptian soldiers marching in rows was found in a tomb.

Banquets

Wealthy Egyptians often celebrated special occasions with extravagant banquets. Friends were treated to fine meals consisting of meat, vegetables and fruit. Servants were on hand to serve food and drink and to provide musical entertainment.

Queen Nefertari is depicted here playing a board game.

Pastimes

In their spare time most men, including the pharaoh, enjoyed hunting and fishing. Women took pleasure in playing music and dancing. Children played many outdoor games that are still enjoyed today such as catch, tug-of-war and leapfrog.

Guests came to banquets in their finest clothes. Some wore wigs topped with incense cones which gave off a pleasant fragrance.

Colourful balls made of clay were filled so that they rattled when tossed.

Religious Festivals

Religious festivals were often celebrated by moving the statue of a god or goddess from its temple and parading it through the streets and along the Nile. Ordinary people flocked to see the statue which was kept locked in the temple during the rest of the year.

This detail from a wall painting shows the creator god Khnum on a ceremonial boat being pulled along by priests.

Fun, Feasts and
Festivals

The Egyptian year was divided into three seasons based on the annual cycle of the Nile. The first season, called *akhet,* was the time of the flood; the second season, called *peret*, was the time for sowing crops; while the third season, known as *shemu,* was harvest time. Festivals were held throughout the year to celebrate religious occasions, the harvest, the flood and other events.

This calendar with hieroglyphs shows the three seasons divided in rows.

Music

Music was a popular form of entertainment and also accompanied religious ceremonies. A range of instruments were played, including the harp, lyre, lute, flute and sistrum (a metal rattle used during temple services). Music was not written down so musicians had to learn songs by heart.

The lyre was a popular instrument.

The Calendar

The Egyptian year was made up of 360 days. It was divided into 12 months of three weeks each (10 days per week). Five extra days were added at the end of each year. According to Egyptian belief, these were the days on which Osiris, Isis, Horus, Seth and Nephthys were born. They were considered holy.

For a long time modern scholars were unable to read ancient Egyptian writing. Then a stone was found with the same text repeated in two Egyptian languages and ancient Greek. A French scholar used this to decipher the Egyptian languages.

24

This paint palette was used to decorate papyri and probably belonged to an important official.

Scribes used pens and brushes made from reeds.

Writing

Hieroglyphics was the oldest of the three ancient Egyptian scripts. The word hieroglyph comes from the Greek and means "sacred carving". This script was mainly used for official and religious purposes. The second script, called hieratic, is simpler and was used for everyday purposes. The third, demotic script, was even simpler. It was developed later than the other two and used from the 7th century BC.

Knowledge
and Education

Very few children went to school in ancient Egypt so most people could not read and write. Professional scribes kept accounts and wrote legal documents and letters. Texts about architecture, trade, medical matters, law and much else have been found. These documents show how science and magic were not separate for the ancient Egyptians as they are for us, but mixed together.

Important events in the life of Amenhotep III were written on the back of this charm in the shape of a beetle.

Scribes

Only a few boys from wealthy families were trained as scribes. They held an important position in society and were highly regarded. Many scribes worked as local officials or with the army, organising supplies and recording events. Others became architects or clerks to wealthy families. The most successful scribes served as teachers in temples or became scholars.

Education

Only a few boys learned how to read and write. They started school at the age of five and usually studied for 12 years. Lessons were held in buildings near temples or outdoors. Students also studied maths and foreign languages, such as Babylonian. Sport and exercise were also part of the school day.

This papyrus contains a hieroglyphic hymn to the hawk-headed sun god, Ra.

Books of the Dead

Illustrated *Books of the Dead*, with spells, charms and magical passwords were placed in coffins. It was believed that the knowledge they contained was essential for the dead to pass through the underworld and reach a happy afterlife.

Young boys learned hieratic script first, writing on pieces of pottery or limestone.

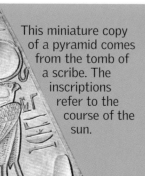

This miniature copy of a pyramid comes from the tomb of a scribe. The inscriptions refer to the course of the sun.

Technology

Unlike the Babylonians or the Greeks, the Egyptians were not great mathematicians or inspired scientists. However, they were keen observers and kept accurate records. This enabled them to predict the yearly flood and to invent their calendar (the basis of ours). Their ability to measure with great accuracy allowed them to build the pyramids.

The falcon god Horus was associated with the planets Jupiter, Saturn and Mars.

Irrigating Fields

The Egyptians used a mechanical tool called a shaduf to irrigate their fields. It was a long wooden pole fixed on a post with a bucket hanging from a rope at one end and a weight at the other. The bucket was lowered into the river, filled with water and then swung around to water the field.

This detail from a tomb painting at Thebes shows a man using a shaduf to water his vegetable garden.

Herdsmen drove their cattle past the tax collectors who would count them and determine how much tax was due.

Paying Taxes

Most farmers and herdsmen were peasants, and like all other Egyptians they had to pay taxes. Since ancient Egyptians did not use money, taxes were paid with corn. At harvest time government officials would visit each district to figure out how much was due. The amount that was owed in taxes depended on how good the harvest was that year.

Many tomb offerings were in the form of food, such as these gift baskets, containing cumin and juniper berries.

Farm Animals

Sheep and goats were kept for meat, as well as for wool and skins. Cows were raised for their meat and milk, while geese and ducks provided eggs. Animals were also kept on farms to do the hard work. Oxen were used to pull ploughs while donkeys carried heavy loads.

Egyptians used simple ploughs which were heavy spikes that cut long, narrow tracks in the soil.

Farming
and Food

A farmer's life, like the Egyptian calendar, followed the annual cycles of the River Nile. The year began with the flooding of the lands, which made the dry desert fertile. During this time little farm work was done. Then when the waters receded, farmers planted their seeds. The end of the year, which was the dry season, was a busy time too. It was during this time that crops were harvested.

Diet

Aside from the meat provided by farm animals, the Egyptians also hunted wild animals, such as gazelles and hares, and caught fish in the Nile. Fruit and vegetables were also a big part of the diet. Lettuce, onions, beans and turnips as well as figs, dates, grapes, pomegranates and melons were grown.

Harvest workers separated grain from its outer casing by bashing it and then throwing it in the air. The wind then blew away the lighter casing, leaving the heavier grain to fall to the ground.

This wooden model shows a man brewing beer which was made by soaking stale bread and barley cakes in water.

Cereals

The most important crops were wheat and barley. These were used to make bread, a staple food for rich and poor alike. Another fundamental food was beer, the ancient Egyptians' favourite drink. It too was made from cereals.

This jewel, made of gold, lapis lazuli and turquoise, was found in a pharaoh's tomb. The eye, represents the eye of Horus, which was believed to keep evil away.

Jewellery

Ancient Egyptian craftspeople made fine jewellery for the wealthy using all sorts of materials, including gemstones like lapis lazuli, turquoise and amethyst. Poorer people wore simpler jewellery. Since most people were buried with their jewels, many pieces have survived.

Bottles and vases containing make-up and perfumes were stored in chests like this one.

Hairstyles

Children and young people had their heads shaved leaving just a lock of hair which was worn hanging down the side. Some men shaved their heads completely while women usually wore their hair long. Wigs were popular, especially for women.

People took good care of their hair, keeping it clean and neatly combed.

Clothing
and Jewellery

The ancient Egyptians spent lots of time taking care of themselves. It was important to keep clean and to look one's best. People went to great lengths to make sure that their fine white linen clothes stayed that way. Wealthy people wore jewellery, make-up, perfume and wigs. Banquets and special events were perfect occasions for dressing up. As in other societies, beautiful clothing and jewellery were a way of showing wealth and status.

Perfume and Make-up

Both women and men used make-up and perfume. Black powder and green paint worn around the eyes was made from minerals. Lips were also coloured red using a paste made from rusted iron.

Perfumes were made from oils.

An animal-shaped perfume container.

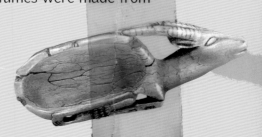

Making Fabric

Most clothing was made from white linen. Linen was light and comfortable in the hot desert climate. Stems and fibres of the flax plant were spun to make thread. Women then wove the thread on looms to create large pieces of linen fabric.

These model sandals of gold, made as a tomb offering, give us an idea of what ancient sandals looked like.

Women used wooden spindles to twist fibres into thread.

Clothing

Clothing styles did not change much over the thousands of years of Egyptian history. Clothing was generally simple and loose-fitting. Workers who spent hours under the hot sun wore simple loin cloths. Children also wore very little or nothing at all. Wealthy people wore long garments of the finest linen. Dyed fabrics were introduced in later times.

Only high-ranking priests and priestesses, like the woman shown here, wore garments made from leopard skin.

These tablets, written in the Akkadian language, are letters sent between Egyptian rulers and their officials in faraway lands discussing trade and diplomatic missions.

The first Egyptian coins were not minted until the 4th century BC. Coins minted at Memphis were used to pay Greek soldiers who helped the Egyptians fight against the Persians.

Neighbours

In times of peace, ancient Egyptians traded with African peoples and all over the eastern Mediterranean and across the Red Sea. Some of its major trading partners were Syria, Canaan, Lebanon and Yemen.

Traded Goods

Local merchants, as well as foreign traders, brought their goods to riverside markets which became ancient Egypt's shopping centres. These traders are bringing wildfowl and wine.

Egyptians traded by exchanging goods of equal value. They dealt with other kingdoms in Africa as well as in the Middle East. Grain, papyrus and linen were the main Egyptian exports. Nubia was a source of gold, cattle and slaves. Myrrh, herbs and spices, leopard skins, dogs and baboons came from the land of Punt. From the Middle East the Egyptians obtained wood and gemstones.

Trade Routes

Much trade was carried out by boat, but the Egyptians also sent huge trading caravans across the desert. To reach trade routes in the Red Sea, they carried parts of ships across the eastern desert and assembled them again when they reached the coast.

Larger sea-going vessels, like this merchant ship, were developed to make the transport of heavy cargo possible.

Cattle, sacks of grain, and other supplies are brought on board a Nile boat.

Trade

The Egyptians transported grain, cattle and other goods up and down the River Nile in sturdy boats. They also sailed into the Mediterranean Sea and traded with the peoples living around its shores. Through trade the Egyptians were able to acquire goods they needed. Although trade brought wealth, it also attracted invaders, hungry for Egypt's riches.

Foreign Rule

Egypt fell to the Persians in the 6th century BC, and was conquered again by the Greek leader Alexander the Great in 332 BC. Alexander founded a Greek city, called Alexandria, to be the new capital of Egypt. His successors, the Ptolemies, ruled Egypt for 300 years. After the Ptolemies, Egypt was taken over by the Romans, who absorbed the lands into their empire. Lasting almost 3,000 years, ancient Egypt was one of the longest-lasting and most brilliant civilizations the world has ever known.

Bust of a Ptolemaic ruler.

This glass goblet, with a Greek inscription around the top, was found at a religious site in Upper Nubia.

Index